LEVEL
2

Dolphins

Melissa Stewart

NATIONAL
GEOGRAPHIC

Washington, D.C.

For Claire
—M.S.

Published by the National Geographic Society, Washington, D.C. 20036. All rights reserved.
Reproduction in whole or in part without written permission of the publisher is prohibited.

Library of Congress Cataloging-in-Publication Data
Stewart, Melissa.
Dolphins / Melissa Stewart.
p. cm.
ISBN 978-1-4263-0652-5 (pbk. : alk. paper) — ISBN 978-1-4263-0653-2 (library binding : alk. paper)
1. Dolphins—Juvenile literature. I. Title.
QL737.C432S73 2010
599.53—dc22
2009022832

cover, Photolibrary.com; 1, Stephen Frink/ Digital Vision/ Getty Images ; 2, Mauricio Handler; 4, Konrad Wothe/ Minden
Pictures; 6, Carlos Eyles; 7, David B. Fleetham/ SeaPics.com; 8-9, Brandon Cole; 10, Carlos Eyles; 12-13, Doug Perrine/
SeaPics.com; 14, Wolcott Henry/ NationalGeographicStock.com; 15, Miriam Stein; 16-17, Hiroya Minakuchi/ Minden Pic-
tures; 18-19, Doug Perrine/ SeaPics.com; 19 top, Ingrid Visser/ SeaPics.com; 20, Florian Graner/ naturepl.com; 20 inset, Uko
Gorter; 21, Doug Perrine/ SeaPics.com; 21 inset, Uko Gorter; 22, Kevin Schafer; 23, Todd Pusser/ naturepl.com; 24, Michael S.
Nolan/ SeaPics.com; 25 top, Joao Quaresma/ SeaPics.com; 25 bottom, Roland Seitre/ SeaPics.com; 26-27, Brandon Cole; 28,
Leandro Stanzani/ Ardea.com; 29 top, Phillip Colla/ SeaPics.com; 29 center, Doug Perrine/ SeaPics.com; 29 bottom, Kevin
Schafer; 31, Bob Couey/ SeaWorld/ Getty Images; 32 top left, Brandon Cole; 32 center left, Leandro Stanzani/ Ardea.com; 32
bottom left, Carlos Eyles; 32 center right, Leandro Stanzani/ Ardea.com; 32 bottom right, Doug Perrine/ Seapics.com;

Printed in the United States of America

Table of Contents

It's a Dolphin!   4

Fish or Mammal?   6

A Dolphin's Life   8

Under the Sea   14

Where Dolphins Live   18

What's the Difference?   20

Super Dolphins   24

Goofing Off   28

Dolphins and Humans   30

Picture Glossary   32

It's a Dolphin!

What swims
in the water,
but isn't a fish?

What whistles
and chirps,
but isn't a bird?

What loves to jump,
but isn't a frog?

It's a **DOLPHIN!**

Fish or Mammal?

A dolphin is a mammal—just like you.

Dolphins have lungs and breathe air. They get oxygen through a hole on top of their heads.

Their tails move up and down.

They have soft, smooth skin.

A dolphin's body temperature is always about 97 degrees Fahrenheit.

OXYGEN:
An invisible gas in air and water that animals breathe in.

MAMMAL:
A warm-blooded animal that drinks milk from its mother and has a backbone and hair.

Dolphins look like fish, but they are different in some very important ways.

Fish have scales.

Fish have gills. Gills help fish get oxygen from the water.

Their tails bend from side to side.

A fish's body temperature matches the temperature of the water it's in.

A Dolphin's Life

A baby dolphin
is called a calf.

A baby dolphin has a small
mouth. The calf smacks
food against the water to
break it into bite-size bits.

A calf can swim as soon as it is born. It drinks milk from its mother's body. When the little dolphin is about six months old, it starts to eat fish.

Water Words

CALF:
A young
dolphin

9

A dolphin pod

Dolphins live in small groups called pods. Some pods join together to form schools. A dolphin school may have more than 1,000 animals.

Dolphins use squeaks, squeals, and whistles to "talk" to each other. Some dolphins in a pod are in charge of watching for sharks and other predators.

Every dolphin has its own name. Each name is a series of whistling sounds.

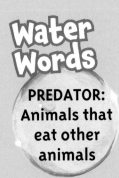

Water Words

PREDATOR: Animals that eat other animals

Dolphins work together to catch prey. Dolphin pods will swim circles around a school of fish until the fish are tightly packed together.

PREY: Animals that are eaten by other animals

This big group of fish is called a "bait ball." When the fish have nowhere to escape, the dolphins take turns diving in for a snack.

Under the Sea

A dolphin's body
is just right for
life underwater.

Flippers help a
dolphin start,
stop, and turn.

The fin on a
dolphin's back helps
it stay balanced.

Its powerful tail pushes it
through the water.

When a dolphin swims slowly,
it rises to the surface and breathes
once or twice a minute. When a
dolphin swims fast, it leaps out
of the water to catch its breath.

Blowhole

When a dolphin breathes out, air blasts out of its
blowhole at 100 miles an hour.

Dolphins have great eyesight, but the ocean can be very dark. It's hard for dolphins to see the little fish they like to eat on the ocean floor.

If a dolphin is hunting alone, it will put its head to the ground and make a clicking noise.

The noise hits anything in the dolphin's path and bounces back. A dolphin can find a fish by seeing it with sound!

This dolphin is using echolocation. You say it like this: eck oh low kay shun. Dolphins actually use echoes to locate the fish they can't see.

Where Dolphins Live

More than 30 different kinds of dolphins live on Earth.

Most dolphins swim in warm ocean waters near the Equator. But some live in cooler seas north and south of the Equator, and some even live in rivers.

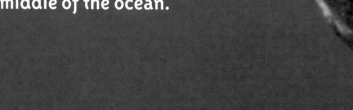

The hourglass dolphin lives way out in the middle of the ocean.

The Hector's dolphin usually stays close to land.

Water Words

EQUATOR: An imaginary line halfway between the North and South Poles.

What's the Difference?

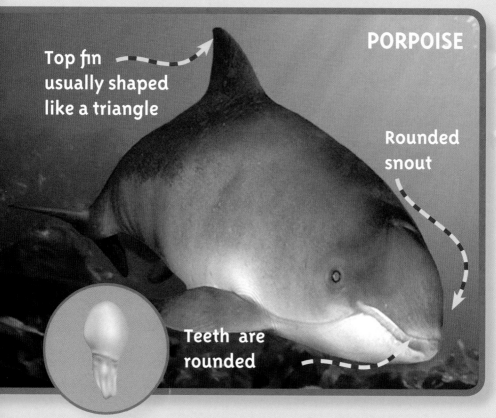

PORPOISE

Top fin usually shaped like a triangle

Rounded snout

Teeth are rounded

Have you ever seen a porpoise? It looks like a dolphin, but it's different. You say it like this: poor pus.

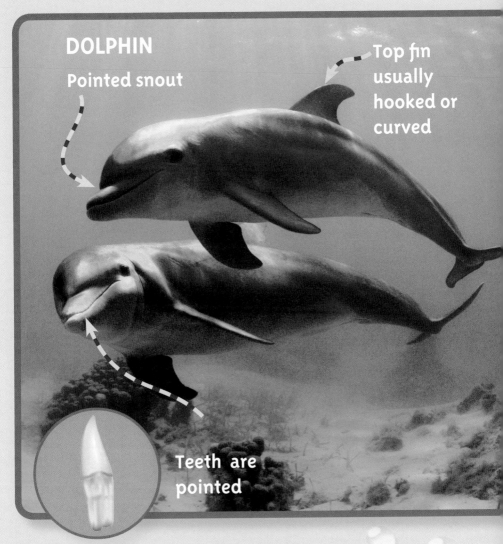

DOLPHIN

Pointed snout

Top fin usually hooked or curved

Teeth are pointed

A dolphin's body is longer and leaner than a porpoise's body. Dolphins are more curious and playful, too.

21

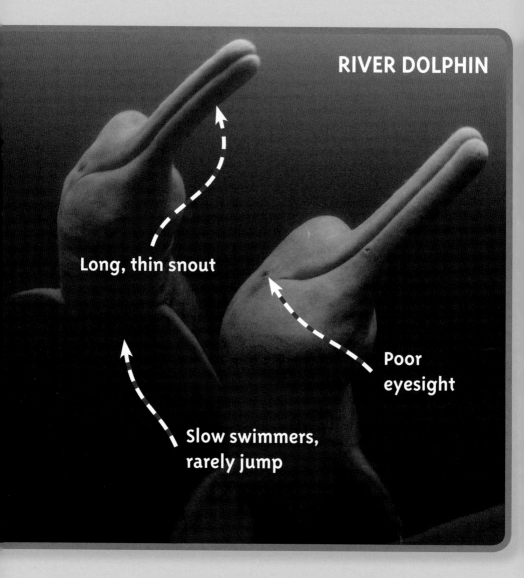

RIVER DOLPHIN

Long, thin snout

Poor eyesight

Slow swimmers, rarely jump

Have you ever seen a dolphin with a long pointy snout? This funny looking mammal is a river dolphin.

OCEAN DOLPHIN

Good eyesight

Short snout

Fast swimmers, often jump

River dolphins are smaller than their ocean-swimming cousins. They are also less active and playful.

Super Dolphins

SUPER SPINNER
A spinner dolphin twirls through the air like a spiraling football. It can jump almost ten feet into the air and spin up to seven times.

Q What is a spinner dolphin's favorite amusement park ride?

A The merry-go-round.

EASY BREATHER

A dolphin spends most of its life holding its breath. A Risso's dolphin can go for 30 minutes without coming up for air.

DEEPEST DIVER

Whales and dolphins are very closely related. In fact, some animals we call whales really are dolphins. The long-finned pilot whale is a dolphin that can dive almost 2,000 feet!

The most amazing dolphin of all is the **ORCA,** also known as the killer whale. The orca wins almost every record-setting award in the dolphin category.

A killer whale can swim seven times faster than an Olympic swimmer!

Q What did the ocean say to the killer whale when it left on vacation?

A Nothing. It just waved.

HUNGRIEST
An orca eats everything from sea turtles and penguins to seals and sharks.

LONGEST LIVING
A killer whale can live up to 90 years.

BIGGEST
Males can grow almost as long as a school bus.

Goofing Off

Dolphins spend a lot of time hunting for food. And they are always on the lookout for danger. But sometimes dolphins just want to have fun. Dolphins make up all kinds of games.

PLAYING CATCH: Toss seaweed into the air and try to catch it.

SURFING: Ride along storm waves or waves breaking near a beach.

TAG, YOU'RE IT: Chase each other through the water.

Dolphins and Humans

Dolphins are gentle, playful creatures. They are also very smart, which is why people and dolphins get along so well.

By learning about these friendly marine mammals, humans are helping to protect dolphins and the waters they live in.

CALF: A young dolphin

Equator

EQUATOR: An imaginary li halfway between the Nort and South Poles

MAMMAL: A warm-blooded animal that drinks its mother's milk, has a backbone, and hair.

OXYGEN: An invisible gas in air and water. It helps anim get energy from food.

PREDATOR: Animals that eat other animals

PREY: Animals that are eat by other animals